MIND GRAPES

WE ALL FEEL A LITTLE NUMB SOMETIMES AND THAT'S OKAY

PRAGATI JAIN

notionpress.com

INDIA • SINGAPORE • MALAYSIA

ISBN

Hardcase 979-8-89588-269-6
Paperback 979-8-89544-847-2

Acknowledgements:

This book is dedicated to a younger me who was once lost.

A special shout out to my family and friends for loving me unconditionally. I am deeply grateful to have you all in my life.

SADNESS AND HEART BREAK

In the cafe around the corner,

I saw you smiling at your significant other,

My breath fell short and my scars started to burn,

For I thought, you'd be my forever!

In the cafe around the corner,

I saw you kissing your significant other,

My eyes started to tear up and I wondered,

If you were ever this happy when we were together?

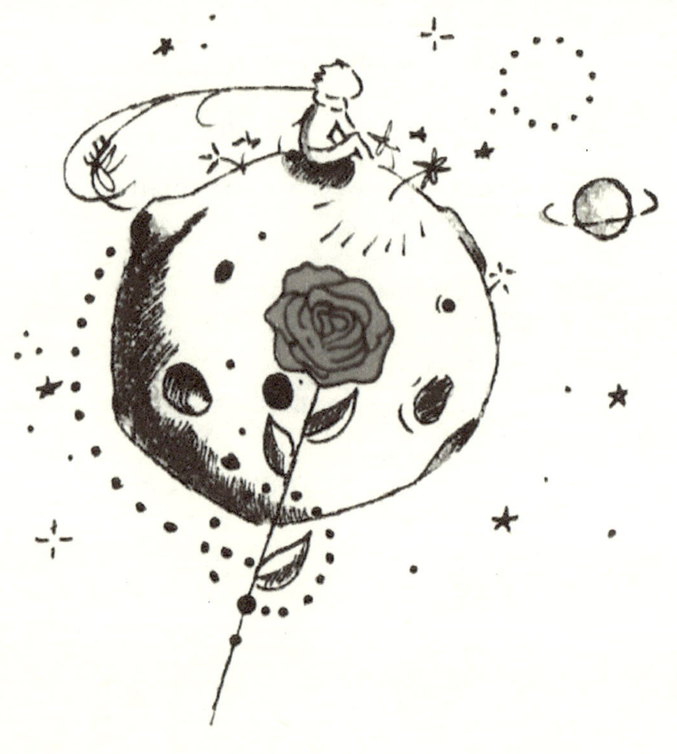

Sad days pass by,

But they leave a broken me behind,

Everyone but me seems to have forgotten the guilt of bidding some of the hardest goodbyes.

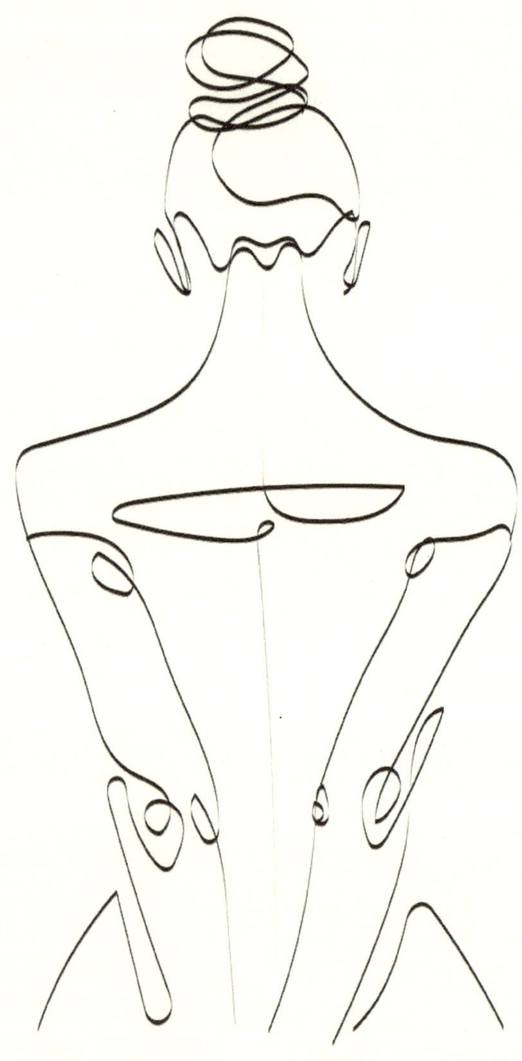

Debased myself with all my insecurities,

Drowned my sorrows with regret and fear,

Pulled my confidence down with judgment and grief,

Killed my dreams piece by piece,

Behold the enemy inside of me,

For it is the one that still controls each part of me.

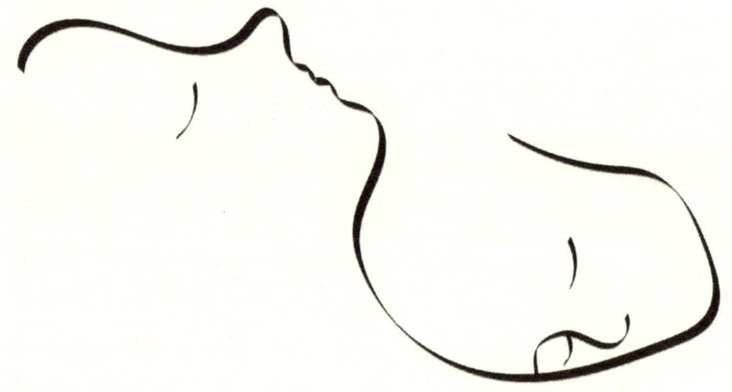

If I tell you that I'm not okay,

Would you tell me that I'll be alright someday?

If I tell you that I feel all alone,

Would you hug me and tell me that you'll always be here and won't ever go ?

If I ever complain about my weight,

Would you tell me that I'm better that way ?

If I tell you that I'm broken on the inside,

Would you tell me that you'd still love me till the end of time?

Living in the past is what I do best,

How do you not go back to relive what you once forgot to cherish?

How do you let go of the friendships lost somewhere in time?

How do you accept that your favourite people moved on, leaving you behind?

It's comforting to know that there once was a time, when a happier me really did live her life.

Nowhere to call home,

Nobody to phone when she's all alone,

Scared of growing up,

Terrified of change,

What if all her decisions were a big mistake?

Tired of fighting her trauma each day,

Wondering if she would ever make it her own someday.

Pent up and grim,

Nobody to blame, but my own self

Lost in a way, I can't seem to define

There's a certain kind of relief in pain that I always seem to find.

Perhaps my poignant sense no longer hopes and loves the melancholy of the present.

Lonely cities and unsolicited thoughts,

These repressed emotions bring forth an untamed storm,

Unsure of what comes next,

Adulting isn't as easy as they said,

Keeping up appearances with a void inside,

A certain emptiness keeps eating me alive.

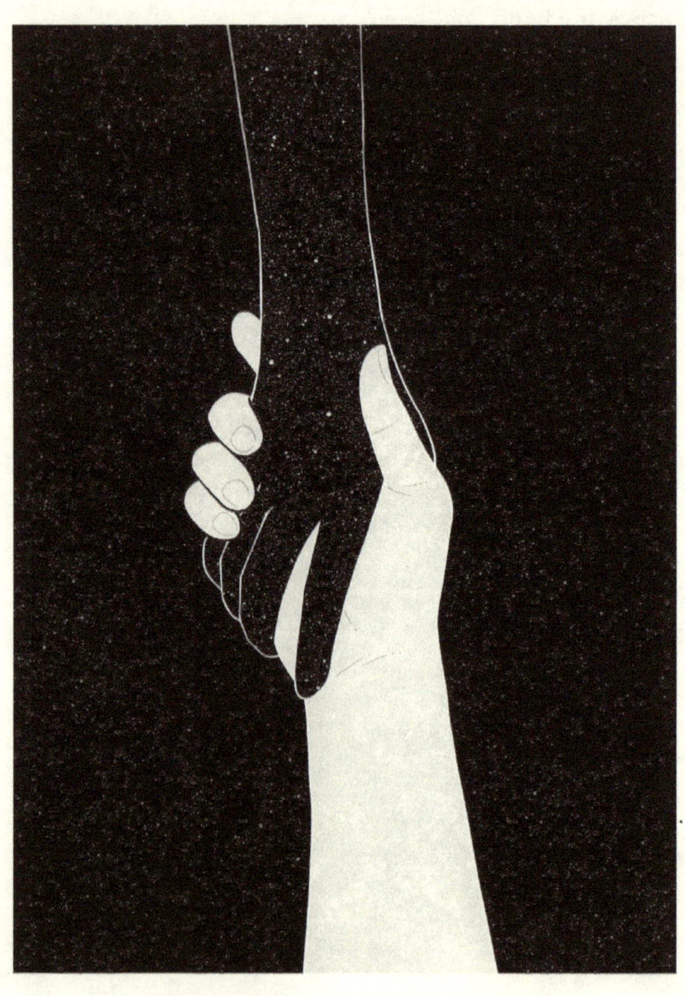

Mundane Days woven into a destined life,

Stuck inside this head, is a string of unpleasant lies,

I take a step forward and then 2 steps back,

Moving on isn't as easy as they said,

Yes, change is scary but so is the past,

Stuck in between a choice of altering thoughts,

Wanted to let go a couple of hundred times,

But didn't want to take away the faint memories that I kept with me all this while,

Always stayed true to what I said,

Never thought you'd be the one to outwit,

Perhaps the world didn't agree with our happiness,

Or maybe I was the one blinded by your sweet tenderness.

Empty castle,

Hollow walls,

Still reminiscing the time past,

Full of pride,

Wanting somebody to come and stay deep inside,

Standing tall and majestic,

Wishing for a glimmer of light to shine bright on it's dark and lonely insides.

You tore me apart like I meant nothing,

You left me on the sidewalk still choking,

A part of me died that day,

A part of me wanted to run away,

Never thought I would live to see myself this way,

Wish I could warn my younger self,

Wish I could tell her that this isn't how your story ends.

Deep within all the answers scream,

Perhaps I am the one too scared of the truth.

In a room full of people, all I feel is loneliness,

My body's finally given up, feeling ashamed of itself,

My brain never stops thinking about my life goals,

My heart still awaits for "the one",

My memories creep in somehow to relive the friendships bygone,

How is it possible to feel soo much all at once and not want to give up?

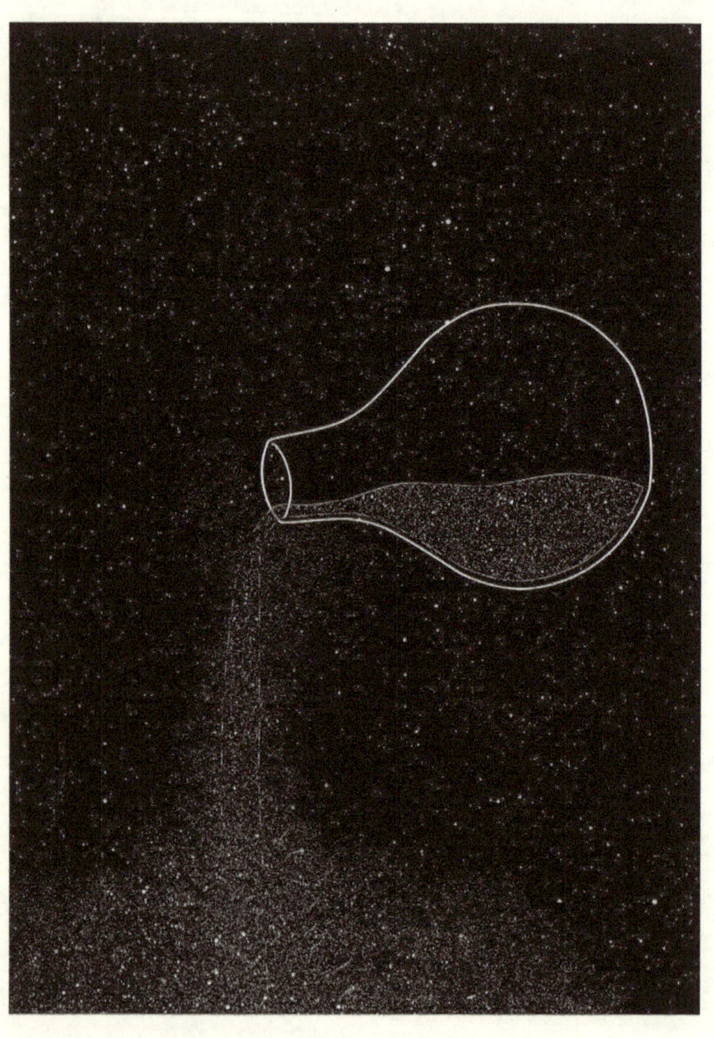

Drowning, just a little bit more each day,

Drowning in my head,

Drowning in my thoughts,

Drowning in emotions,

Drowning in my pain.

Faded memories,

Clouded Feelings and nagging pains,

My wrecked self sinks each day,

The hopes behind these shattered pieces will find an escape someday.

Sorrows of the past keep weighing me down,

My long lost warmth calls me out,

I keep pushing and pulling to let love in,

But my imprisoned self burns in agony and consumes me from within.

For all the tired things you say on repeat,

For all the broken conversations you try to keep,

For all the lies that continue in between,

Perhaps our forbidden love was never meant to be.

I want to be lost in the midst of nowhere,

Lay down under the stars and talk about a million things that were left unsaid.

Unreal promises and surreal hopes,

I always find myself chasing onto bigger goals,

Muddled lives and Deja Vu's

Brawny desires but woeful truths.

Not sure what I am looking for,

Nothing quite seems to fit,

Functioning with a void inside,

Reassuring myself that I'll survive,

Thought I had erased all the memories from the past,

But they keeping gushing back like waves from an ocean afar,

Need somebody to tell me that I'm not alone,

Need somebody to tell me that this too shall pass.

Haven't felt those butterflies since you left,

Haven't felt the same gush of emotions I used to get,

Have I not moved on or have I just accepted the reality?

Maybe in an alternative universe we're still together,

And maybe in that alternative universe you really did make the right decision,

Wish you were here with me sometimes,

Wish I could still tell you about the tiniest details of my life,

Not sure why but I still look out for you,

Wish I could erase that one night somehow,

Wish that I could've found out before I fell for you.

Saw myself from a distance for a long time,

Wishing I could change everything about my life,

Not sure how I landed here,

Would other choices have changed my present for the better?

Do you ever regret the things you did?

Did you ever realise that what you were doing wasn't the best?

Would you ever go back to make it right?

Or would you prefer to leave it at a goodbye instead?

Bruised and Abandoned,

Just left to be,

Kept on suffocating,

No one to set me free.

Woeful Eyes,

Tattered Smiles,

Bandaged pieces of a harrowing life,

Shadows cast,

Delusional hearts,

Left astray with no way out.

Misjudged and a Misfit,

Broken into a thousand pieces,

I keep calling out,

For someone to finally hear me out loud,

Left in the middle of nowhere,

My anxious self is desolated and in despair,

All I ever do is just wonder,

Will there ever be a light at the end of this tunnel?

Replaced identities,

Misplaced emotions,

Recreating a familiar pattern,

Tortured and held on the inside,

Awaiting freedom with nothing but hopeful eyes.

Abused and Tortured,

Ran down and Belittled,

My crippled self often wonders,

Will I ever get a do over?

Choose isolation, not confinement and you will breathe easier.

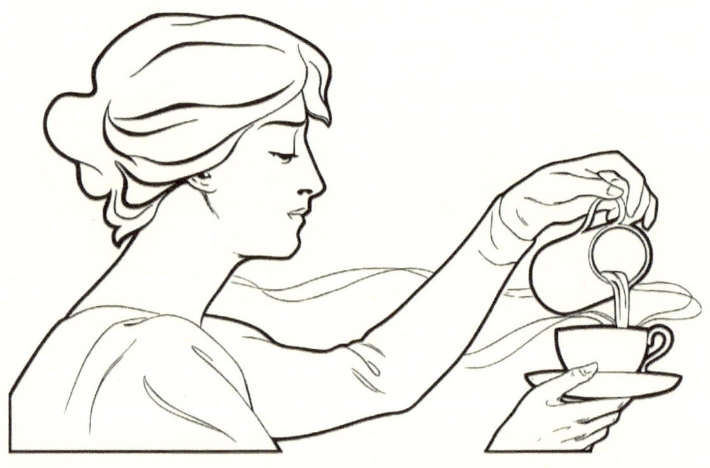

Internal pains and bruises end up becoming our worst enemies. They hurt the most and usually come without any cure.

The matters of my heart remain unexplained,

The scepticism in my tone never seems to fade.

Replayed the situation in my head a gazillion times,

But alas, came to the same conclusion every time.

I remember making fake scenarios in my head, only to escape the horrid realities of my present.

Wished I could unlearn what had happened,

Wished I could still fit myself back into that toxic situation.

A part of me died that day.

A missing piece that remains lost somewhere in time.

Years past and I admitted defeat,

Because it started to feel like maybe I was just squandering through my life.

It was then, when I realised, that in my failed attempts to find that old, misplaced piece,

I actually found a new and improved me.

I started to notice how much I had changed for the better,

I now understood emotions at a deeper level.

I now find solitude in the most chaotic messes of my life.

Perhaps, it really is true what they say,

"That healing never comes linear"

Faces over Faces,

People after people,

A thousand similar conversations which seem to go nowhere,

Been questioning myself a lot lately, why do I put up with this misery?

Is it all in the name of seeking that one heartfelt connection or have I just grown to find solace in these repetitive patterns?

What is love really ?

Maybe a delusion that becomes an absolute goal in life.

An urban legend that sends you onto a goose chase for a long long time.

I think the real question here is, when does one finally loose the tiny glimmers of hope and decides to quit?

I hope you know that I did give it my all,

I hope you know I left everything, just to give us a real shot.

Ghosts of us wherever I go,

Ugly reminders of everything we would do,

I used to believe they would eventually fade away with time,

But I guess, I was the one who learned to live with them one day at a time.

I wanted to win you so bad that on the way I lost myself completely.

You were the one I always wanted. Little did I know I was a choice you never made.

Yes, I was angry because it was the only way I could still keep a part of you with me. But I realise now, that I need to let you go to set me free.

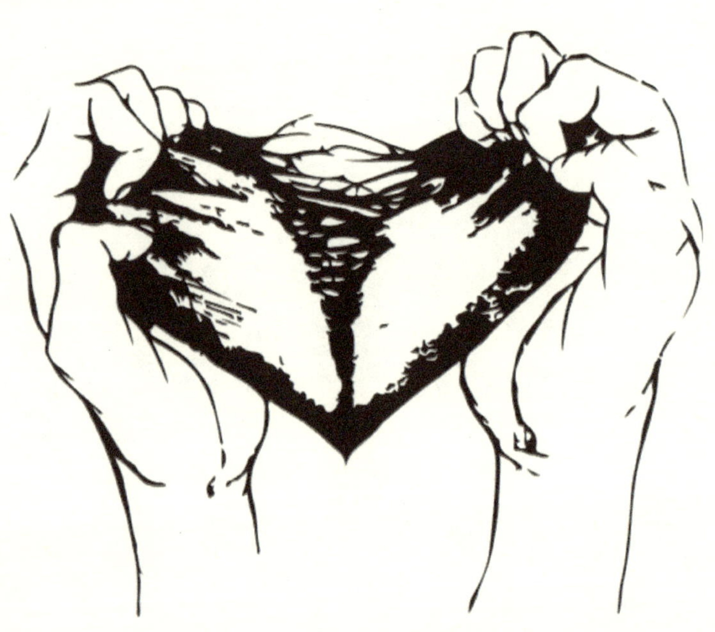

In between all my life goals, ambitions and plans, you were just a very messy decision.

Somewhere between a heartfelt connection and destiny, distance crept with a nasty ulterior motive.

In the moonlight,

under the stars

you grabbed my hand and took me afar,

Into the woods,

behind a tree,

You told me that we were meant to be,

My nervous heart started to wonder,

Perhaps you're the one that would last forever.

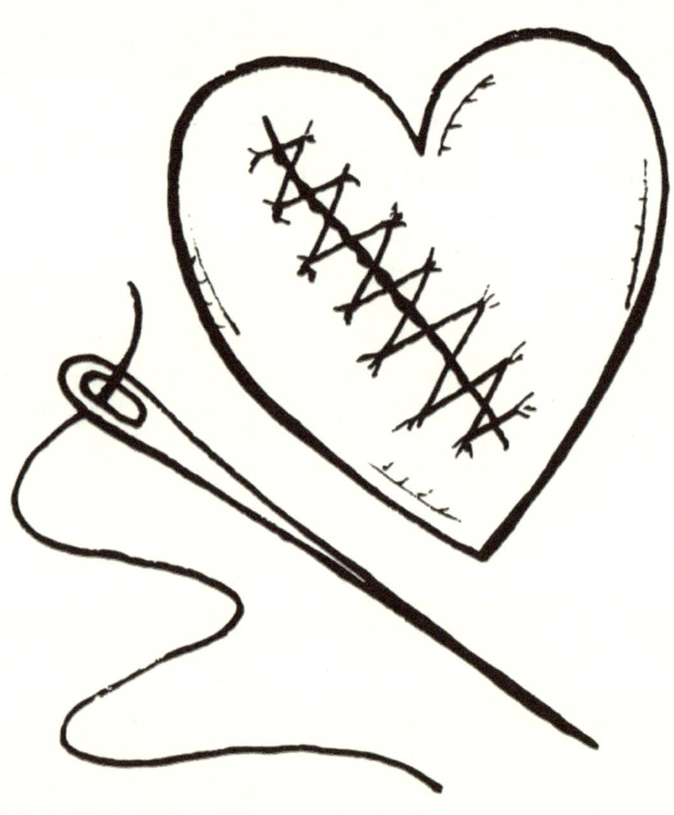

Familiar feelings, burning desires.

Same old promises, Hesitant gestures.

Distant memories, Fearful heart.

Do you really want to run back to what was never yours?

And when we finally meet each other again,

I hope that we're the best versions of ourselves.

The versions that are ready to dive into the deep end,

The versions that aren't afraid of their emotional baggage anymore,

The versions that really were meant to be.

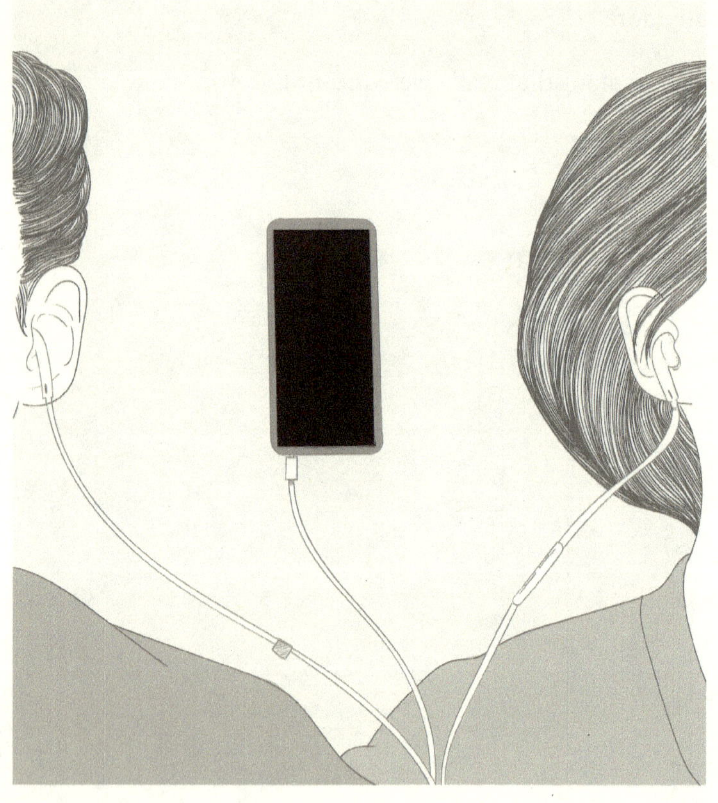

Time heals everything they said,

But honestly it brings back similar situations instead.

You'll find yourself going through the same rush of emotions again,

You'll find yourself smiling at those silly texts again.

Would you give it a fighting chance this time or would you rather just try to hide your feelings deep inside?

love

It beats,

It breaks,

It loves,

It aches,

Only and only for you.

My barren heart grows no more,

The reigning demons within me have let go of all hope,

These drowning, consuming thoughts in me, defeat me each night and won't ever set me free.

You'll find yourself travelling back in time when you hear that old song or when you smell an old perfume on someone new.

The ghosts from the past run right back into your head.

Even though it's just for a second, you'll notice yourself smiling, just dwelling on the time past, how far you've come and how painful it was leaving somebody back in time, just buried to be missed as nothing but a sweet old memory that's well kept inside.

Hiding in the confines of my fears,

I feel left out and cornered,

I often close my eyes and wonder,

Will I ever survive the terror?

Pretending to fake a smile,

Make small talk to reassure ourselves we're still the same while we both know deep within our hearts that the space between us was real this time. It's unfair how temporary separations can create permanent distances.

HEALING

From time to time,

We all need to let light in,

Take a leap of faith and jump back right in,

Only this time, it's to love our own damn selves.

Decided to turn my sorrows into strength and make my misery blossom into my greatest success.

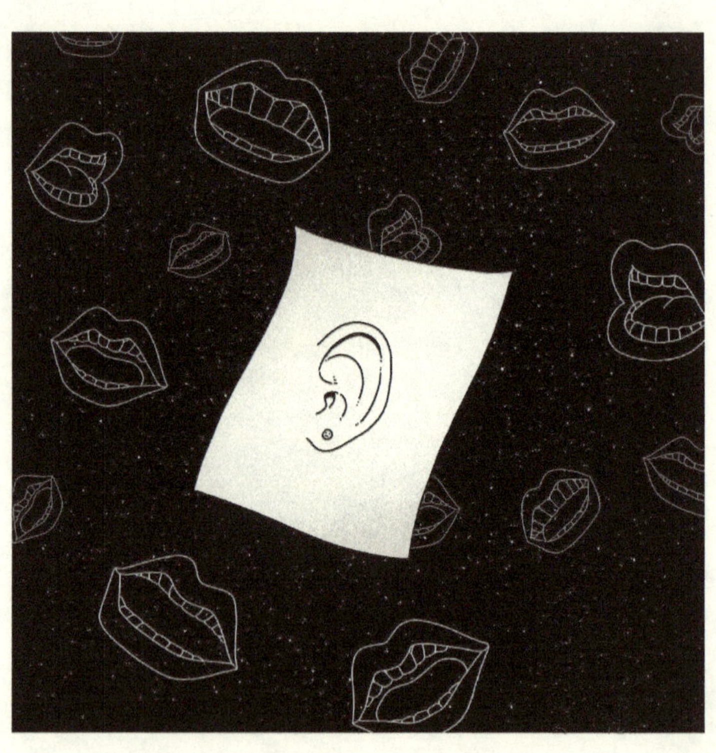

While everyone else is busy bringing me down.

I thrive, I thrive each day and let my success do all the talking.

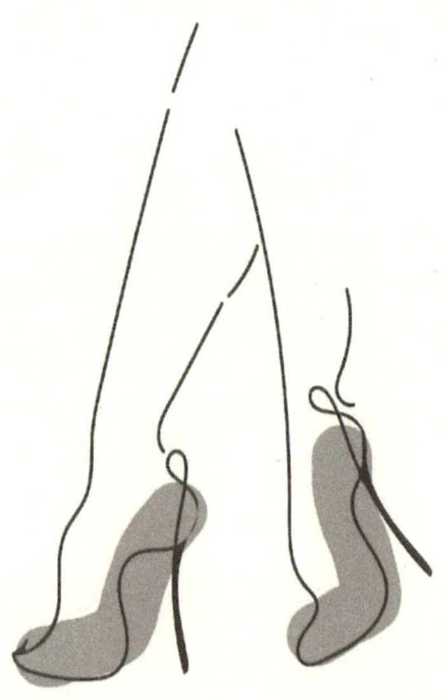

Stepping up and Climbing,

Rising up and Shining,

The stabs in my back are just scars,

Reminding me of my journey so far,

The hustle is real,

But the surreal view from up here,

Was worth all the trouble.

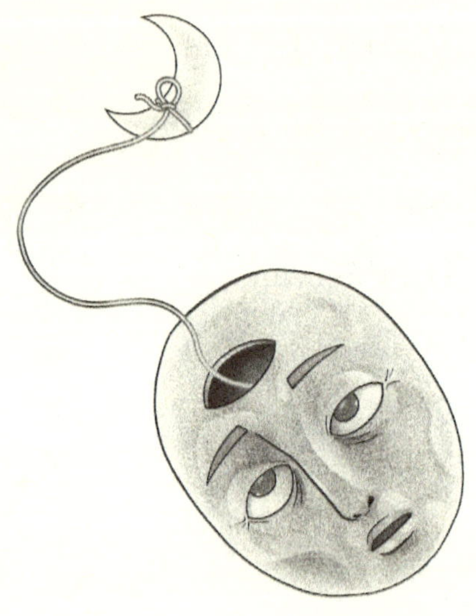

At the end of the day, it all starts and ends with your own mind,

If you let it grow inside of you,

It will always hold power over you.

And just like that, I picked up the shattered pieces of me and saw through the reflection of my inner strength and power.

A part of me is still as naive as it was at 13,

A part of me is still as hopeful as it was at 15,

A part of me is still as heartbroken as it was at 18,

A part of me is still as dispirited as it was at 23,

As much as I try to heal, these parts of me will still remain like war marks on an army chief,

They will sneak up on me in the most unexpected moments,

So at 25, my goal is just peace. I embrace all of me, forgive myself and everyone else that hurt me.

Letting go isn't easy but at 25 my priority is just me.

www.ingramcontent.com/pod-product-compliance
Lightning Source LLC
La Vergne TN
LVHW091108150826
845673LV00002B/745
* 9 7 9 8 8 9 5 4 4 8 4 7 2 *